Henry Lewis, Jonathan Sayer and Henry Shields

Peter Pan Goes Wrong

Third Edition

methuen | drama

LONDON • NEW YORK • OXFORD • NEW DELHI • SYDNEY

METHUEN DRAMA
Bloomsbury Publishing Plc
50 Bedford Square, London, WC1B 3DP, UK
1385 Broadway, New York, NY 10018, USA

BLOOMSBURY, METHUEN DRAMA and the Methuen Drama logo are
trademarks of Bloomsbury Publishing Plc

First published 2014
Reprinted 2015 (twice), 2017 (twice), 2019

Adaptation published with permission from
Great Ormond Street Hospital Children's Charity

A catalogue record for this book is available from the British Library.

A catalog record for this book is available from the Library of Congress.

ISBN: PB: 978-1-4742-9165-1
ePDF: 978-1-4742-9166-8
ePub: 978-1-4742-9167-5

Series: Modern Plays

Typeset by Mark Heslington Ltd, Scarborough, North Yorkshire
Printed and bound in Great Britain

To find out more about our authors and books visit www.bloomsbury.com
and sign up for our newsletters.

Peter Pan Goes Wrong was first presented by Mischief Theatre Ltd on 10 December 2013 at the Pleasance Theatre in London with the following cast and creative team:

Chris	Henry Shields
Robert	Henry Lewis
Francis	Harry Kershaw
Sandra	Charlie Russell
Dennis	Jonathan Sayer
Max	Dave Hearn
Annie	Sophie Whittaker/Nancy Wallinger
Trevor	Rob Falconer
Jonathan	Greg Tannahill
Lucy	Daisy Waterstone
Writers	Henry Lewis, Jonathan Sayer & Henry Shields after J.M. Barrie
Director	Adam Meggido
Assistant Director	Andy MacNamee
Designer	Martin Thomas
Lighting Designer	Owen Evans
Sound Designer	Ella Wahlström
Choreographer	Nell Mooney
Co-composer	Richard Baker
Co-composer	Rob Falconer

The production was then presented by Kenny Wax Ltd and Stage Presence Ltd on a national tour in 2014/15 with the following cast and creative team:

Chris	Laurence Pears
Robert	Cornelius Booth
Sandra	Leonie Hill
Max	Matt Cavendish
Dennis	James Marlowe
Trevor	Chris Leask
Francis	Harry Kershaw
Annie	Naomi Sheldon
Jonathan	Alex Bartram
Lucy	Rosie Abraham
Male Understudy	Fred Gray
Female Understudy	Laura Kirman
Director	Adam Meggido
Set Designer	Simon Scullion
Lighting Designer	Matt Haskins
Costume Designer	Roberto Surace
Sound Designer	Ella Wahlström
Co-composer	Richard Baker
Co-composer	Rob Falconer
Assistant Director	Sita Thomas

The touring production transferred to the Apollo Theatre in London's West End for the Christmas 2015–2016 season with the following cast and creative team:

Chris	Henry Shields
Robert	Henry Lewis
Francis	Tom Edden
Sandra	Charlie Russell
Max	Dave Hearn
Dennis	Jonathan Sayer
Annie	Nancy Wallinger
Trevor	Chris Leask
Jonathan	Greg Tannahill
Lucy	Ellie Morris
Male Understudy	Fred Gray
Female Understudy	Rosie Abraham
Director	Adam Meggido
Set Designer	Simon Scullion
Lighting Designer	Matt Haskins
Costume Designer	Roberto Surace
Sound Designer	Ella Wahlström
Co-composer	Richard Baker
Co-composer	Rob Falconer
Co-choreographer	Dave Hearn
Co-choreographer	Nancy Wallinger

J.M. BARRIE AND *PETER PAN*

All children, except one, grow up

James Matthew Barrie was born in the small weaving town of Kirriemuir, Scotland on 9 May 1860, the ninth of ten children of a handloom weaver. For the first six years of his life, James lived in the shadow of his mother's love for his older brother David. Tragically, on the eve of his fourteenth birthday, David was fatally injured in a skating accident. In his desperate attempt to be loved and to replace David in his mother's life, Barrie virtually became David. Trying so hard to be his brother affected him deeply, and the notion of the everlasting childhood stayed with Barrie and became one of the defining reasons for his lifelong love of children.

Barrie married Mary Ansell, an actress, in 1894 and although they had no children, he had many as friends. In Kensington Gardens in 1897, while walking his St Bernard dog Porthos, Barrie met the eldest three Llewelyn Davies boys, George, five, Jack, four, and Peter, still a baby. Two more sons, Michael and Nico, joined the family in the next few years and Barrie developed a strong friendship with the children and their parents, Sylvia and Arthur.

Sylvia and Arthur both tragically died when the boys were still young. Barrie became their guardian and brought them up as his own children. His life with the boys has been explained as the strongest inspiration for the creation of *Peter Pan* in 1904. Barrie himself once said: 'By rubbing the five of you violently together, as savages with two sticks to produce a flame, I made the spark of you that is Peter Pan.'

The story and play of *Peter Pan* emerged gradually over a number of years. Peter made his first appearance in *The Little White Bird* published in 1902, in a chapter entitled *Peter Pan in Kensington Gardens*, which told the story of how the baby Peter came to Kensington Gardens and learned to fly. Then, in 1903, Barrie sat down to write what was to become *Peter Pan*, although his new play was first entitled *The Great White Father* – a title which, fortunately, was quickly dismissed.

The first production of *Peter Pan* took place at the Duke of York's Theatre in London on 27 December 1904 and was a phenomenal success. The play ran for 150 performances in London and was revived every Christmas for the next 30 years and more. The novel *Peter and Wendy* was published a few years later in 1911 and became an instant bestseller, and has never been out of print since.

It was another twenty-five years before Barrie stunned the world by making his gift of the copyright to Great Ormond Street Hospital for Children in London, in 1929. By that time, two of the Llewelyn Davies boys – George and Michael – had tragically died. It seems the gift was not a sudden gesture, as Barrie had long thought about how he could help the hospital. This exceptional gift meant that all proceeds from his magical tale would thereafter come to the hospital. Though childless himself, Barrie loved children and had long been a supporter of the hospital. As he said in a speech in 1930, 'At one time Peter Pan was an invalid in the Hospital for Sick Children, and it was he who put me up to the little thing I did for the hospital.'

J.M. Barrie died in 1937 and was buried in the family grave in Kirriemuir.

More fairy dust was sprinkled over Great Ormond Street Hospital in 1988, when the House of Lords, prompted by Lord Callaghan, voted for a special clause in the Copyright Designs & Patents Act, which gave the hospital a right to royalty from *Peter Pan* in perpetuity in the UK. More than eighty years since Barrie's gift, the story of Peter Pan's adventures in Neverland with Wendy, Michael, John, Tinker Bell and the Lost Boys, and his battle against his arch-enemy Captain Hook, is still enchanting children and adults alike and is continuing to help towards making the hospital the incredible centre of hope it is today.

Peter Pan Goes Wrong

Adapted from the original stage play by J.M. Barrie

TO DIE WILL BE AN AWFULLY BIG ADVENTURE

Characters of *Peter Pan*

Narrator
Wendy Darling, *a girl from London*
Michael Darling, *her youngest brother*
John Darling, *her younger brother*
George Darling, *their father*
Mary Darling, *their mother*
Nana the Dog, *the Darlings' nursemaid*
Lisa, *the Darlings' housekeeper*
Peter Pan, *the boy who would not grow up*
Tinker Bell, *his fairy*
Tootles, *one of the Lost Boys*
Captain Hook, *the Captain of the* Jolly Roger
Mr Smee, *his boatswain*
Starkey, *his first mate*
Bill Jukes, *one of his crew*
Cecco, *another of his crew*
Tiger Lily, *a Red Indian*
Crocodile

Actors of the Cornley Polytechnic Drama Society

Trevor *is the company's stage manager and lighting and sound operator*
Chris *is the president of the drama society and plays Mr Darling and Captain Hook*
Robert *plays Nana the Dog, Peter's Shadow and Starkey*
Francis *plays the Narrator and Cecco*
Sandra *plays Wendy Darling*
Dennis *plays John Darling, Mermaid and Mr. Smee*
Annie *plays Mrs Darling, Lisa, Tinker Bell and Tiger Lily*
Max *plays Michael Darling, Mermaid and the Crocodile*
Jonathan *plays Peter Pan*
Lucy *plays Tootles*
ASMs *two of Cornley's stagehands*
Paramedic

The action takes place on opening night of the Cornley Polytechnic Drama Society's production of Peter Pan *adapted after J.M. Barrie by Susie H.K. Brideswell.*

Production Notes

A few notes from the writers about the piece.

With this play-within-a-play you have the slight complication of the actors performing *Peter Pan* and the characters within *Peter Pan*. To try and make it a little simpler the names are laid out in two lists: first the ACTORS, the members of the Cornley Polytechnic Drama Society who are putting on the play; and second the CHARACTERS of *Peter Pan*. The text always specifies and refers to the ACTORS rather than the CHARACTERS.

The stage direction 'vamp' denotes improvised dialogue to cover something. In our experience less is always more with this, but also finding believable improvised lines for your versions of the actors is important and for that reason we haven't included specifics from the original production.

/ denotes the next line beginning over the current line.

Peter Pan Goes Wrong is designed to work on two levels: first, the classic tale of *Peter Pan* which must be allowed to emerge from the disasters and mishaps within the piece and, second, the story of the ACTORS performing the play which should shine through the cracks in their performances throughout to serve the underlying meta-narrative. Everything in the show should be played for truth and not for laughs – when it goes wrong it hurts!

We've found that with this piece it is important to remember that not all of the ACTORS in the play are 'bad actors' but simply the victims of circumstance – the comedy comes from their unwavering endeavour to continue and their optimistic belief that their luck can always change.

The same is true of the set, costumes, lighting, sound and other elements of the production. Everything that goes wrong should be a choice and everything that doesn't go wrong should go right (or in the case of the physical production look right). The better the production looks the more of a journey there is to the complete destruction that is caused in the later stages.

Act One

The stage is set with a large revolve split into three sections. The first displayed to the audience as they walk in depicts the first scene of the play, the Darling family nursery, beautifully decorated with closed doors stage left and stage right leading to the hall and service quarters of the house. A large window is set into the stage left wall. An ornate three-tiered bunk bed stands stage right with a bedside table next to it with a candle standing on it. A wooden train is on the floor. A large toy-chest stands stage right. Three sconces protrude from the walls, currently unlit. The only light on the stage is moonlight which streams in through the window.

In the preshow the theatre lights flicker and fizz occasionally.

Trevor's *tech box sits at the side of the stage surrounded by laptops, sound boards, etc.*

The house music fades out and **Trevor** *steps forward holding a glass bottle of beer by his side. He silences the audience and reads from a sheet of paper.*

Trevor Alright, ladies and gentlemen, welcome to *Peter Pan*. A couple of announcements. The venue kindly requests that patrons ensure they have decanted all drinks into plastic cups.

Realises and hides his beer.

And also that all members of the audience switch off their mobile phones.

His mobile phone rings. He quickly answers it.

Not now, Tanya, I'm on stage. Yeah the audience are in, yeah alright I'll get a photo. Bye.

Hangs up, turns around and takes a selfie shot of himself in front of the audience. We hear the phone camera noise.

(*Continues reading.*) Do also remember that photography of any kind is strictly prohibited. One final note, please be aware that the emergency fire exits . . . are locked. Enjoy the show.

He exits to his box. The house and stage lights come down. **Chris** *and* **Robert** *enter from the stage right wing. A spotlight comes up on them.*

Chris   Good evening, ladies and gentlemen.

Robert   Boys and girls.

Chris   And welcome to the Cornley Polytechnic Drama Society's Christmas production of J.M. Barrie's classic . . .

Robert   *Peter Pan*!

Chris   Please allow me to introduce myself; I am Chris, the director.

Robert   And I'm Robert, the co-director.

Chris   Assistant director. We're hugely excited to present *Peter Pan* as this year we've managed to secure a much larger budget than usual thanks to a sizeable donation from the uncle of one of our cast members, Max. This generous cash . . .

Max *enters from the wings.*

Chris   Thank you, Max, thank you, Max.

Max *goes.*

Chris   This generous cash injection has meant that tonight's production will certainly outshine last year's rather underfunded Christmas show that Robert directed: *Jack and the Bean.*

Robert   But we are optimistic for tonight's pantomime . . .

Chris   It's not a pantomime, Robert, it's a traditional Christmas vignette.

Robert   Oh no it isn't.

Chris   . . . hahaha. It's true we've had several productions where the vision just hadn't been fully realised.

Robert   In one of Chris's productions, due to an ill-timed haircut Rapunzel had to be imprisoned in a bungalow.

Chris   Indeed that was almost as bad as when Robert insisted on using a real cat in his production of *Puss in Boots*, which became known among the society as *Puss Who Was Occasionally in Boots, But Often Refused to Wear His Boots, and Pooed in Them*.

Robert   But this year everyone has come together and we even have my young niece Lucy to play the Lost Boy Tootles.

Chris   Absolutely, who we are sure will overcome her chronic stage fright this evening. We have taken every possible precaution to ensure the smooth running of the show.

Robert   Including a top of the range radio headset for our actor Dennis to ensure he remembers his lines correctly.

Chris   Don't tell them about the headset.

Robert   Well, it's true, Chris, he doesn't know a single line. It's certainly undermined past productions; like when he played the title role in *Oliver!* In the workhouse scene he got up, walked over to Mr Bumble and said 'Please sir, I'm full'.

The company enter with placards and stand in a row behind **Chris** *and* **Robert**.

Chris   So it is with huge excitement that we present tonight's production. With no further ado, please put your hands together for . . .

Robert (*comes in too early*)   *Peter P . . .*

Chris   J.M. Barrie's . . .

Robert (*too early again*)   *Peter . . .*

Chris   Christmas classic . . .

Both   *Peter Pan!*

The cast turn around their placards to reveal the words 'ACT ONE OF PETER PAN'. *Lights down, all exit. Silence and stillness. Overture music starts up, loud, dramatic and magical.* **Sandra** *(as Wendy) moves into position centre stage in a traditional nightgown. A pyro-flash suddenly fires stage right and* **Francis** *magically appears behind it (as the Narrator in a traditional Victorian suit) holding a large old-fashioned storybook.*

Francis   All children, except one, grow . . .

Another loud pyro-flash suddenly goes off. **Francis** *screams.*

All children, except one, grow up. Wendy discovered that she would grow up when she was very young. She was at a picnic and her mother said the words 'Oh I wish you could stay like this forever', and then she knew.

It is this very Wendy, Wendy Moira Angela Darling, along with her two brothers Michael –

Max *enters (as Michael) in a pink baby-gro.*

Francis   – and John –

Dennis *enters (as John) wearing smart, striped pyjamas, glasses and a radio headset.*

Francis   – who begin our story.

Spotlight comes up just off centre stage, missing the three actors. The three slowly shuffle into the spotlight. Shortly after **Francis** *continues his speech the spotlight slowly moves back to where they were before. The three hurry back into it.*

Francis   The setting is their bedroom, on the third floor of a townhouse in Bloomsbury.

Lights up on the nursery scene. **Max** *and* **Dennis** *toss hoops at a quoits board hung on the door.*

Sandra   Come along, boys! Stop playing around, it's time for you to get into your bedclothes.

Max It's too early for bed, Wendy. You are turning into Mother.

The quoits board falls off the door.

Sandra Well, we are all growing up. We can't be silly children for ever.

She reaches up awkwardly to pat **Max** *on the head.*

Sandra Besides, I should love to be like Mother.

Dennis (*we hear some faint radio feedback from his headphones*) Well, I shouldn't. That would be ever so dreary, Wendy.

Max John's right. I can't stand being cooped up in this boring old nursery. I'm four years old.

Dennis (*holds headset*) We're young boys, we should be outside climbing trees and playing with toys.

He drops his yo-yo. It isn't attached to the string and rolls along the floor and off stage.

Sandra Not every day can be an adventure, Michael. Now let's get ready for bed. I can hear Father's footsteps.

Chris *enters (as Mr Darling) followed by* **Annie** *(as Mrs Darling), both in evening dress.* **Chris**'s *tie is untied.*

Chris Has anyone seen my cufflinks?

Annie Oh, George, you are forever losing things.

Lights shift to **Francis**.

Francis Their father George Darling was a man of business; a little pompous, but with a kind heart.

The cast restart the scene.

Chris I have searched . . .

Francis *continues.*

Francis He was far less serene than their mother Mary Darling, a genteel and elegant woman.

The cast restart the scene.

Chris   I have sear . . .

Francis *continues.*

Francis   Although sometimes he forgot to show it, George loved them all dearly.

Long silence. Lights shift back.

Chris   I have searched the house high and low, Mary. I put a thing down for a moment and it is as if fairies have danced off with it.

Sandra   Oh, Father! I would so love to have fairies skipping about the house.

Chris   I don't believe in fairies. I believe in cufflinks.

Dennis *(holds headset)*   Won't you come and play with us, Father?

He rolls a ball at the skittles. It bounces off and we see the skittles are glued down.

Max   Bravo, John. A full score.

Chris   I don't have time for silly games.

Max   You are so serious, Father.

Chris   Grown-ups have to be serious and little children ought to be. Wendy, have you seen my cufflinks?

Sandra   No, Father.

Chris   I mean really, is it me? Or is the world going mad?

He hangs his jacket up on a hook on the wall, but the hook is just painted on and the jacket falls to the floor. He touches the hook and sees it is painted on.

Annie   I'll look in the drawing room, George.

She exits through the stage left door.

Dennis (*holds headset*) Perhaps Nana has seen them, Father.

Chris That creature is almost certainly the reason they are missing.

Lights shift to **Francis**.

Francis It's probably true to say that the Darlings are the only family in Bloomsbury, and probably all of London, to have a dog as a nursemaid. She was a loyal and hardworking Newfoundland named Nana.

Lights shift back and **Robert** (*as Nana the dog*) *enters through a dog flap in the stage right door, in a dog costume with his face exposed. He trips over the flap as he comes in.*

Robert Woof!

Sandra, **Dennis** *and* **Max** Nana!

Sandra, **Dennis** *and* **Max** *pat* **Robert**.

Chris I don't understand all this affection towards that dreadful animal. What about me? Where are my cufflinks?

Sandra Perhaps Lisa has seen them.

Lights shift to **Francis**.

Francis The final member of the household was Lisa, the Darling's housekeeper, different in every way to Mrs Darling.

Lights shift back. **Annie** *enters through the stage left door now dressed completely differently (as Lisa).*

Annie I have found your cufflinks, Mr Darling. You left them on the dresser.

Lights shift to **Francis**.

Francis A sweeter family you've never seen, with hearts as good as gold,
And on this fateful evening, our story shall unfold.

His chair slides sideways off stage and he throws a handful of glitter up as he goes. Lights shift back to the scene.

Chris   Thank you, Lisa. You have saved my evening. I couldn't have gone to the work party without them.

Annie *exits.*

Chris (*chuckles*)   I suppose I am, Lisa.

Annie *re-enters quickly.*

Annie   You are a forgetful man, Mr Darling.

Chris (*chuckles*)   I suppose I am, Lisa.

Annie *exits again and* **Chris** *begins to tie his tie.*

Chris   Now leave that beast alone the three of you.

Dennis   We're only petting her, Father.

He strokes **Robert** *and the head comes off his costume.*

Chris   That dog needs to be taught some discipline. Oh, this tie will not tie! Not around my neck, around the bedpost, oh yes! Twenty times around the bedpost, but around my neck, no sir!

Max   What's wrong, Father?

Chris (*calls off*)   Mary, this is a nightmare! If I cannot tie my tie, I cannot go out this evening, if I cannot go out this evening, I can never go to the office again and if I can never go to the office again I shall lose my job and our children shall be flung out into the streets!

Annie *enters now dressed as Mrs Darling.*

Annie   George, really! Allow me to tie it.

She begins to tie **Chris's** *tie.*

Chris   Now all of you, time for bed and to take your medicine.

Max   I shan't take my medicine, Father.

Dennis (*holds headset*)   We must take our medicine, Michael.

Annie *pulls* **Chris**' *tie far too tight. He tries to continue without showing the discomfort.*

Chris (*constricted*)   Thank you, Mother. Perfectly tied.

Annie   My pleasure, George.

Chris *begins to try and remove his tie.*

Sandra   You must take your medicine.

Max   But it hurts my throat, Wendy!

Chris (*constricted to the point of being barely audible*)   Hurts your throat does it?

Sandra   You must take your medicine, otherwise you shan't grow up to be like Father.

Chris *flails around wildly trying to remove his tie.*

Max   I don't want to be like Father.

Chris (*even worse – desperately clutching at his tie*)   Ungrateful child!

He manages to cut through his tie and gasps for breath, exhausted.

(*Forced calm.*) Really, Michael, what an unnecessary fuss you're making. Fetch the medicine bottle, Nana.

Robert *bangs his head on the dog flap. It only opens outwards so he stands and walks out through the door.*

Chris   When I was small, I used to thank my mother and father for giving me my medicine!

He trips over the wooden train and **Dennis** *moves it out of the way by the stage right door.*

Chris   I would say 'Thank you kind parents! Thank you for giving me bottles to keep me well!'. Ah, here is Nana now.

Max *sits.*

Chris   Hand me the medicine bottle, Nan . . . Hand me the medicine bottle . . . hand me the . . .

Robert *puts the medicine bottle in the wooden train and rolls it across the floor to* **Chris**.

Chris   Thank you, Nana. Now fetch me a spoon.

Robert *tries to squeeze back out through the dog flap, but can't. He struggles harder to get free.*

Dennis (*holds headset*)   Why don't you take yours first, Father?

Chris   Nonsense, John, you shall take yours first and then I shall take mine.

Annie   Boys must take their medicine.

She exits through the stage left door.

Chris   Quite right. Here is Nana with the spoon now. Bring it to me, there's a good dog.

Robert *is still stuck in the door with no spoon; he struggles even harder to get free.*

Max   Here's the spoon, Father.

He gives **Chris** *the scissors to use as a spoon.*

Chris   Thank you, child. Come along John.

He pours the medicine through the handle of the scissors onto the floor.

Dennis (*improvised*)   I don't want it, Father.

Chris (*improvised*)   None of us wanted this.

Dennis *opens his mouth.* **Chris** *slowly puts the handles of the scissors inside* **Dennis's** *mouth and pulls them out. Quiet radio feedback is heard again.*

Dennis   Yuk.

Chris *pours more medicine into the scissors again.*

Chris   Your turn, Michael. Medicine for the clever boy who found the spoon.

*He slowly puts the scissors into **Max**'s mouth. He tries to pull them out but they are stuck. He finally yanks the scissors out and accidentally stabs himself in the leg. He screams in pain.*

Robert   Woof! Woof!

Sandra   Oh look, Father, Nana is excited! Get down off the bed.

Chris *pulls the scissors out of his leg.*

Chris   Oh you useless animal! You've gotten dog hairs all over my trousers!

*He goes over to **Robert** and rubs his trousers over him.*

Sandra   Silly hound! You've gotten hair all over everyone.

*They all rub themselves on **Robert**.*

Chris   You daft animal. I always had misgivings about having a dog as a nursemaid.

Sandra   Father, Nana looks after us so well.

Chris   I am sick and tired of everyone coddling that dog! Does anybody coddle me? Oh no! Well, enough is enough. I'm sick of my children being treated like puppies.

He slips on the medicine. He quickly stands back up.

It's time for that dog to go out where it belongs, in the yard. Lisa!

Annie *enters now dressed as Lisa through the stage right door smashing **Robert**'s face into the toy-chest; she is holding a spoon. She closes the door.*

Annie   Yes, Mr Darling?

Chris   The spoon! Thank you, Lisa, it's a little late! We used the other one. Now take that wretched animal outside and chain her to her kennel!

Annie   Come on, Nana, outside.

She opens the door, again smashing **Robert**'s *face into the side of the chest. She closes the door to reveal* **Robert** *looking even more dazed. He continues to try and get loose.* **Chris** *puts his jacket over* **Robert** *to hide him.*

Chris   Thank God that animal's gone.

Max   Listen to her barking down there.

Robert *barks as if from a distance. Radio feedback sound.*

Dennis   She is unhappy, Mother

More feedback sound.

Father.

Sandra   That is not Nana's unhappy bark; it is how she barks when she senses danger.

Chris   Danger? What possible danger could there be in here?

A sandbag falls from the rig to the floor with a loud crash as **Annie** *enters, dressed as Mrs Darling, through the stage left door.* **Chris**, **Sandra**, **Dennis** *and* **Max** *all cower in the bed.*

Annie   What's all this commotion, George?

Chris   Mary, my dear. Nothing's wrong, the children were just getting into bed.

Annie   Where's Nana?

Sandra   Lisa locked her outside.

Annie   George! But she protects the children.

Chris   Protects them from what?

Annie   The boy who visits this room.

Chris   What nonsense.

Sandra *gets out of the bed and* **Chris** *follows.*

Sandra   Mother and I saw him the other evening; he slipped away through the window. Mother ran to slam it shut before he could escape but he was too nimble, the window shut and we caught just his shadow, which started dancing across the room.

Chris   A dancing shadow? Oh really! What will you come up with next?

Annie   I had Lisa lock it in the chest. See for yourself, George. Lisa has the key.

She exits through the stage left door.

Sandra   Lisa!

Annie *opens the stage left door now dressed as Lisa.*

Annie   Yes, Miss Wendy?

Sandra   Have you the key to the chest?

Annie   I shall fetch it at once.

A car horn is heard outside.

Your cab's here, Mr Darling.

Chris   Excellent, let's go do . . .

Another car horn is heard.

Annie   Another cab's here, Mr Darling.

Chris   Excellent, let's go down . . .

Another car horn is heard.

Annie   A third cab's here, Mr Darling.

Chris   *Three* cabs? (*Looks to* **Trevor** *in the tech box.*) One for Mary . . . one for me . . . and one for . . . my hat. Let's go downstairs.

Annie   I shall fetch the key, Miss Wendy.

Sandra   Thank you, Lisa.

Annie *exits through the stage left door.*

Chris   Mary, the cab's here!

Annie *enters through the stage left door, dressed as Mrs Darling.*

Annie   The cab's here? I shall fetch my shawl.

She exits through the stage left door.

Chris   Very good, Mary.

Sandra   Where is that maid? Lisa!

Annie *enters through the stage left door, dressed as Lisa but with one arm trapped in the costume, holding the key.*

Annie   I found the key, Mr Darling.

Sandra   Now I can show you the shadow, Father!

Chris   Oh, Wendy, you really must grow up. There is no shadow.

Annie *opens the chest and takes out the shadow.*

Chris (*not looking*)   I don't have time for this. That will be all, Lisa.

Sandra   Please look, Father!

Annie *exits through the stage left door.*

Chris   Mary, the cab's here, we shall be late!

He opens the stage left door, **Annie** *is midway through getting changed; she covers herself and* **Chris** *quickly closes the door. He reopens it and* **Annie** *is changed, now wearing her Mrs Darling costume, but without her shawl.*

Annie   Yes, George, I found my shawl.

The shawl is thrown onto her.

Chris   Ah very good! Come along, Mary!

Sandra *puts the shadow back in the chest.*

Sandra   The boy who the shadow belonged to was accompanied by a ball of light, no bigger than my fist, but it darted around the room like a living thing.

Chris   I don't believe it for a moment. I'm going downstairs! Someone has to be grown-up around here.

He opens the stage right door but can't get past **Robert**. *He climbs up over* **Robert** *and slides through the gap. His foot disappears last, but the door pulls his shoe off. He reaches through and takes it.*

Annie   Alright, my dears, time to turn the lights off. Make sure you all . . . *oh*!

Max   What is it, Mother?

Annie   I thought I saw . . . a face at the window, nothing there.

Trevor *walks past the window with a large power-saw. Realises. Hides from view.*

Annie   Must be my imagination.

Max   Mother, I am glad of you.

Annie   I am glad of you too, Michael.

Dennis (*holds headset*)   Will you sing us a lullaby, Mother?

Radio feedback sound.

Dennis   No, Dennis, speak with feeling. No don't repeat that, you idiot.

Annie   Of course, my sweet.

She beautifully sings a lullaby to the children as she lights the candle and places it on the end of the bed.

Annie (*sings*)   Hush now, my Darlings, don't you stir. Dream of a world of adventure.

As she sings she pulls the drawstring on the sconce by the bed. It goes out. She pulls the drawstring on the next one and it goes out. She goes to the third sconce and pulls the string; it goes out and the second sconce comes back on. She turns the second sconce off again and the third one comes back on. She pulls the third drawstring again; it goes out and the second sconce comes on again. She pulls the second sconce off the wall.

(*Sings.*) Be at peace, you'll be grown-up one day
   'Til then put your fears away.
   Out of sight and out of mind
   I tidy the worries I find.
   Softly sleeping while I sing,
   Be safe in the world dreaming brings.

Trevor *begins to saw* **Robert** *out of the door.* **Annie** *sings louder to compete with the sound. An* **ASM** *comes on with a hammer to help. Another* **ASM** *joins with a chainsaw. Eventually* **Robert** *is freed and the team exit.* **Robert** *exits taking a section of the door with him.*

Annie (*sings*)   Close your eyes and rest your heads,
   Safely tucked up in your beds.
   All is quiet and all is calm.
   I'll never let you come to harm.
   Nightlight lit to guide the way,
   Until the sun brings in the day,
   And as they take their maiden flights,
   Guard my sleeping babes tonight.

She finishes the lullaby.

Max   That was beautiful, Mother.

Annie   Thank you, my dear.

She places the candle on the post of the bunk bed.

Sandra   Can anything harm us when the nightlight is lit?

Annie   Nothing, precious.

The top bunk of the bunk bed falls onto the middle bunk sharply, trapping **Max**.

Annie   They are the eyes a mother leaves behind her to guard her children.

Max (*muffled under the top bunk*)   Mother, you look so pretty tonight.

Annie   Are you tucked in, Michael?

Max (*under the top bunk*)   Yes, Mother!

Annie   Are you comfortable?

Max *lifts up the top bunk with his feet and arms.*

Max   Yes, Mother.

Annie   And you, Wendy?

Sandra   Yes, Mother.

Max *drops the top bunk, which crashes down on him. In turn his bunk crashes down onto* **Dennis***.*

Annie   And, dear John, are you feeling sleepy?

Dennis *lets out a muffled scream.*

Annie   Goodnight, my Darlings.

She lights a candle on the end of the bed.

Dear nightlight that protects my sleeping babes burn clear and steadfast tonight.

She tries to exit through the stage right door, but it's jammed. She crawls through the hole **Robert** *left. The lights dim. Tinkling music plays. A light suddenly appears in the window. It darts around the room, searching for something.* **Trevor** *wanders on and we see he is making the light with a laser pen. He realises his mistake and steps offstage. The lights then disappears through the keyhole of the chest. Bells are heard within the chest. The light re-emerges from the chest and disappears through a crack in the stage left doorway. Silence. Suddenly* **Jonathan** *crashes through the window breaking it and is yanked up and down wildly as he flies into the room. He tries to stand up but is pulled back and knocked into the wall. He stands up and composes himself.*

Jonathan (*whispers*)   Thank heavens I didn't wake the children. Tinker Bell? Tink? Where are you? Have you found my shadow? Do you know where they put it?

Annie *enters from the hall door having changed her costume again (now as Tinker Bell). She is covered in fairy lights and bells and jingles as she walks. As she moves further into the room we see she has a power cable attached to her back which leads offstage. She switches on her fairy lights.*

Jonathan   There you are! Do you know where they put it?

Annie *jingles her bells.*

Jonathan   In the toy-chest? Where?

Annie *jingles her bells and walks over to the chest. Her cable is too short and pulls her back.* **Trevor** *leans onstage unspooling more cable to allow her to move forward.*

Jonathan   In here?

Annie *jingles her bells and points to the chest.*

Jonathan   Are you ready, Tink? Don't let it startle you! It's time to get my shadow back, don't let it dance away.

He goes over to the chest which bursts open and **Robert** *jumps out, dressed in black lycra (as the shadow). Music plays.* **Annie** *exits startled.* **Robert** *dances around the room as the shadow trying to get away from* **Jonathan**.

Jonathan   Aha! Got you! Now to stick you back where you belong. I shall stick you on with soap!

He opens the medicine cabinet and takes out a bar of soap. He rubs it on his and **Robert**'s *feet.* **Sandra** *wakes.*

Sandra   Boy, why are you crying?

Jonathan *remembers and starts crying.*

Jonathan   I'm not crying. What's your name?

Sandra   Wendy Moira Angela Darling. What's yours?

Jonathan   Peter Pan.

Sandra   What are you doing?

Jonathan   I'm trying to stick my shadow back on.

Sandra   You can't stick a shadow back on with soap. It must be sewn.

Jonathan   What is *sewn*?

Sandra   I shall show you.

She takes a needle from her sewing bag and sews the shadow on. She stabs **Jonathan** *in the foot and he yelps.* **Robert** *copies him.*

Sandra   There! It's done! Why don't you try it?

Jonathan *springs up and moves around the room.* **Robert** *copies his motions.*

Jonathan   Wendy, it's done. Look! Look! The cleverness of me.

Sandra   Well, if I did nothing I shall return to bed.

She sits down sharply on the bed. **Dennis** *and* **Max** *groan in pain.*

Jonathan   Wendy, one girl is worth twenty boys.

Sandra   Do you really think so, Peter?

Jonathan   Yes, I do!

Sandra   Well, that's perfectly sweet of you and I shall get up again.

She stands on the bed, making **Dennis** *and* **Max** *groan again.*

Sandra   I'll give you a kiss if you like.

Jonathan   Thank you.

Holds out his hand.

Sandra   Don't you know what a kiss is?

Jonathan   I shall know when you give it to me.

Sandra *gives him a thimble from her sewing bag.*

Jonathan   Now shall I give you a kiss?

Sandra   If you please.

They go to kiss. **Robert** *pushes them apart.*

Robert   Not on stage!

He takes an acorn from the brim of **Jonathan**'*s hat and gives it to him;* **Jonathan** *gives it to* **Sandra**.

Sandra   I shall wear it on a chain around my neck.

She reveals a large acorn already on a chain around her neck.

How old are you?

Jonathan *springs across the room.* **Robert** *tries to copy him.*

Jonathan   I don't know, quite young.

A leap move leaves **Robert** *standing in front of* **Jonathan**.

Robert   I ran away the day I was born!

Sandra   . . . Ran away, why?

Robert   I'll tell you why –

Jonathan *springs across the room again and shoves* **Robert** *out of his way.*

Jonathan   I heard mother and father talking of what I was to be when I was a man. I want always to be a little boy and have fun. So I ran away to Kensington Gardens and lived a long time among the fairies.

Sandra   You know fairies, Peter?

During the next speech **Robert** *becomes tangled in* **Jonathan**'*s flying line, gets it caught around his neck and begins choking. Eventually he is untangled.*

Jonathan Yes, but they're nearly all dead now. You see when the first baby laughed for the first time the laugh broke into a thousand tiny pieces and they all went skipping about and that was the beginning of fairies. There ought to be a fairy for every boy and girl.

Sandra Ought to be? Isn't there?

Jonathan Oh no, children know such a lot now, soon they don't believe in fairies and every time a child says 'I don't believe in fairies', there is a fairy somewhere that falls down dead.

He flies up to the bed. **Robert** *doesn't have a wire, so has to climb up. He tries to leap off the bedside table but it breaks underneath him. He clambers up the bed and stands on the windowsill behind* **Jonathan**.

Sandra You can fly?

Jonathan Of course I can fly!

He springs off the bed and floats gracefully to the floor. As he flies he accidentally kicks **Robert**, *who falls backwards out of the window with a huge crash.*

Jonathan Wendy, come away with me to Neverland!

Sandra Oh dear, I mustn't! Think of Mother, besides I can't fly!

Jonathan I'll teach you.

Robert *re-enters in pain and stands behind* **Jonathan** *again.*

Sandra How lovely! To fly! But is it far?

Jonathan Not far at all, just the other side of the stars.

He gestures to the window. A star cloth pops up outside. **Robert** *copies* **Jonathan**'s *arm gesture but accidentally leaves his arm over the lit candle. His arm catches fire and he panics.* **Trevor** *runs on with a fire extinguisher and puts him out, then leaves.* **Robert** *crawls across the stage and tries to get out through the dog flap but again gets stuck halfway.*

Sandra   Would you teach John and Michael to fly too?

Jonathan   Of course!

Sandra   John! Michael! Wake up! There is a boy here who is to teach us to fly.

Max (*muffled*)   Fly? I should love to fly.

Sandra *and* **Jonathan** *lift the bunk off* **Max** *and he climbs out of the bed.*

Sandra   He shall take us to Neverland!

They drop the bunk sharply and **Dennis** *screams again.*

Dennis (*extracting himself from the bed*)   Neverland?

Sandra *and* **Jonathan** *help* **Dennis** *out of the bunk bed.*

Max   Can you really fly?

Jonathan   Look!

Max   How do you do it?

Jonathan   It's simple, you just need your happiest thoughts and a little bit of fairy dust.

He blows glitter over the three of them.

Sandra   Fairy dust! How delightful.

Two **ASM**s *enter through the two doors. As the stage right door opens it swings* **Robert** *round again and smashes his face through the side of the chest.* **Trevor** *pops up through the toy-chest and he and the* **ASM**s *attach* **Dennis**, **Max** *and* **Sandra** *to their fly lines.*

Max   We're all ready to fly.

Jonathan   Just think of a lovely, wonderful thought and it will lift you into the air.

Max   All together?

Sandra   Yes!

As the **ASM***s and* **Trevor** *exit the stage right door is closed to reveal* **Robert** *with the broken chest panel around his neck. Music begins.*

Sandra One.

All Two. Three.

The fly lines attached to **Sandra**, **Max** *and* **Dennis** *are all suddenly pulled up, but the lines tear off their costumes leaving them all standing in their underwear in a line on stage. Only the top half of* **Max**'s *costume has been torn off. He removes the bottom half in order to match the others.*

Sandra We're flying!

Max I feel light as air!

Dennis (*holds headset*) Whee!

Jonathan It's time to go. Follow me to the window.

The set begins to revolve to reveal a set of the rooftops of London. Music continues. **Jonathan** *lands on the window ledge. A spotlight comes up on him.*

Jonathan Come on Tink!

Tinker Bell's light flickers past the others.

Jonathan Second to the right and then straight on till morning!

Jonathan Here we go!

He leaps off the window ledge and flies over the rooftops. As the revolve turns he is flown straight into the moon, which falls off the set wall, then into a cut-out of Big Ben, which breaks. Music swells and the revolve continues to turn.

Jonathan (*upside down and in pain*) You see! It's easy when you know how!

Max This is tremendous!

Sandra I'm flying!

Dennis (*holds headset*)   Woohoo!

Jonathan   Come on, boys, don't be scared. Come and fly with me!

The other three, in their underwear, all scramble to climb through the window. **Max** *and* **Dennis** *fall hard to the floor behind the rooftops.* **Sandra** *stands in the window.*

Sandra   Look, Michael and John are doing somersaults!

Max *and* **Dennis** *do forward rolls on the rooftops, in their underwear. The music continues as the set keeps revolving.*

Jonathan   This way! Keep up if you can.

He flies off upwards into the rig.

Sandra   Peter, wait for me!

Max   And me!

Dennis (*holds headset*)   And me!

All   Neverland! Here we come!

The set slowly completes its revolve and reveals the forest of Neverland; a beautiful, ethereal forest, covered in glittering flowers. The set consists mainly of two large trees; the one to the stage right side has a red door in the side of it with a wooden ladder leading up to it. The music stops and **Francis** *slides on in his chair, holding his book. He throws glitter.*

Francis   And now we arrive in the forests of Neverland. A world of infinite wonders. Peter and Wendy landed in a forest glade and skipped joyfully through the trees.

So as Peter plays with Wendy
And jealous Tink draws near
Our tale shall continue,
And I shall disappear.

He throws a handful of glitter up in the air again. The chair begins to very slowly slide sideways. He waits, looking out to the audience. The chair stops. Half of him is still visible. The chair begins to move

*out again. His leg gets caught on the tabs and he stops. A hand
reaches out from the wing and moves his leg. He moves off again.
He disappears.* **Jonathan, Sandra** *and* **Annie** *enter from behind
the trees.*

Jonathan   Wendy, look. We're here!

Annie *switches on her fairy lights and we hear an electrical clunk.
All the lights immediately go out plunging the stage into darkness.*

Beat.

Sandra   Oh, Peter, it's beautiful.

*In the darkness she is given a torch which she shines onto
her face.*

Jonathan   You can see all of Neverland from here, Wendy.

Sandra   I've never seen trees quite like these before.

*She shines the torch onto the stage to highlight the set but she shines it
on* **Trevor** *who is in a precarious position trying to pass a torch to*
Jonathan*. They are both startled.*

Sandra *and* **Trevor**   Argh!

Sandra   Peter who is that?

Jonathan   That, Wendy, is Tootles, one of the Lost Boys.

Sandra *moves the torch and shines it on* **Lucy** *who looks terrified.*

Lucy   I'm Tootles.

Jonathan   That, Wendy, is Tootles, one of the Lost Boys.
The other one was a . . . err a mermaid.

Torch shines back onto **Trevor** *who does an impression of a
mermaid. Suddenly the lights snap back on and he leaves.*

Jonathan   Hello, Tootles!

Lucy *stares in silence at the audience. She tries to run off behind the
trees but we briefly see* **Robert** *push her back on.*

Robert   Get back on, Lucy! You're doing it!

Lucy *tries to speak but her nerves make her stammer.*

Lucy   P . . . p . . . p . . . pp . . .

Robert *leans on looking furious and prompts her.*

Robert   Peter!

Lucy   I . . . I . . . I . . . I . . .

Robert   Peter, I have to tell you something!

Jonathan   Oh yes? What is it you want to tell me, Tootles?

Lucy   T . . . t . . . t . . . t . . .

Robert   Come on, Lucy, you're embarrassing me!

Sandra   Come on, Tootles, you can do it.

Lucy   T . . . t . . . t . . . t . . .

Robert   Tinker Bell told me to shoot down Wendy!

Jonathan   Tink did that? Then, Tink, I am your friend no more; be gone from me for ever.

Sandra   Oh, Peter! You mustn't banish her.

Jonathan   Oh well, not for ever but for a whole week.

Annie *storms off behind a tree, the Tinker Bell light re-emerges and they all watch it fly off.* **Annie** *is then seen exiting behind the tree.*

Jonathan   Well done, Tootles.

Lucy   P . . . p . . . p . . . p . . . Peter. Peter.

She looks pleased with herself.

Jonathan   That's right.

Lucy   I . . . I . . . I . . . I ha . . . I have to t . . . tell you something.

She looks happy and relieved.

Robert   Oh for God's sake!

He bangs his hand against the tree and the branch collapses on **Lucy**, *crushing her leg.* **Robert** *sheepishly leaves.*

Jonathan   Well . . . um . . . thank you, Tootles.

Panpipe music suddenly plays. He quickly gets out his panpipes and mimes playing them but is too late and the music stops.

Sandra   Oh, Peter! You play beautifully . . .

Suddenly we hear **Chris, Robert** *and* **Dennis** *singing and growling.*

Jonathan   Pirates! Quickly, into the hideout.

Captain Hook theme music then plays and **Jonathan** *and* **Sandra** *climb up the ladder on the stage right tree. Mist drifts forward.* **Dennis** *(as Mr Smee),* **Francis** *(as Cecco) and* **Robert** *(as Starkey, complete with peg-leg and parrot puppet) enter the stage swinging in on ropes.* **Dennis** *swings in and lands stage left,* **Francis** *swings and lands stage right but* **Robert** *fails to land and swings straight across the stage landing in the wings with a crash. He re-enters with the peg-leg protruding from his knee. He walks normally, then puts his peg-leg down. The music builds to a crescendo as* **Chris** *(as Captain Hook) enters walking through the mist.*

All   Yarr!

Chris   The glorious sound of a deserted forest, Mr Smee.

The car-horn sound effect plays again.

A cab . . .

Francis   Not a soul for miles around, Captain Hook.

Chris *spots* **Lucy**'*s leg which is protruding out from underneath the fallen tree. He pushes the leg out of sight with his foot.*

Robert *(unintelligible through a pirate accent)*   These old dark woods give me the creeps, Cap'n Hook.

Chris   Ay, Starkey. I know what you mean.

Dennis   Captain! We shall find the Lost Boys at . . .

A brief moment of feedback is heard.

You're listening to Classic FM. That was the Violin Concerto in A minor by Johann Bach.

Chris   We shall find the Lost Boys at the Mermaid's Lagoon. You might be right, Smee. Oh how I'd like to slice their gizzards out.

Dennis   What a goal! A dramatic last-minute equaliser.

Chris   Thank you, Smee.

Dennis (*sings*)   Lady in red –

Chris   Thank you, Smee.

Dennis   Dennis, we are experiencing some radio interference, please stop repeating everything you hear. No don't repeat what I've just said. No. Stop it! These aren't lines . . . stop repeating what I'm saying . . . no don't repeat that either . . . stop repeating me . . . Stop repeating . . .

Chris   Thank you, Mr Smee!

He removes **Dennis**'s *headset.*

Chris   But most of all I want Peter Pan! For he cut off my arm, Starkey!

Robert (*unintelligible*)   Disgraceful! That boy has no manners, Captain. Don't you agree, Percy?

He talks with his parrot puppet.

(*unintelligible parrot voice*)   Disgraceful. Disgraceful. I do agree, Starkey! (*Unintelligible pirate voice.*) Ay, Percy knows how it is.

Chris   Exactly. I've waited long to shake his hand with this!

He holds up his hand and the hook falls off. He tries to put the hook back on with difficulty.

Pan flung my arm to a crocodile that happened to be passing by.

Dennis *without his headset forgets his line.*

Chris (*prompts*)   I've often noticed your fear of that crocodile, Captain Hook.

Dennis   I've often noticed your fear of that crocodile, Captain Hook.

Chris   He got a taste for me flesh that day, Mr Smee.

Dennis *forgets his line again.*

Chris (*prompts*)   He's followed you around ever since, Captain Hook.

Dennis (*comes in with Hook's line*)   That he has, Smee, that he has.

Chris   But by lucky chance it swallowed a clock, Captain. So before it can reach you, you hear the clock and bolt.

Dennis   What are you doing with your pistol out, Mr Smee?

He looks at his own pistol.

Chris   I wouldn't want to be caught unawares, Captain.

Dennis   Put that thing away, Smee, or I'll strike you down with my hook.

He grabs **Chris***'s hook.* **Chris** *snatches it away.*

Chris   *No*! Put that thing away, Smee, or *I'll* strike *you* down with *my* hook! *You're Smee.* I'm Hook.

Dennis   I'm John.

Chris   You're *Smee*. But some day the clock will run down! Ah men, the thought of it, tis the only thing in this world that scares me . . .

There is a sudden flash and bang as one of the narrator's pyrotechnics goes off again. **Chris** *jumps.*

Chris   But soon, men, I shall have the foolish boy within my grasp. Ah, revenge is a grand thing!

Robert   Oh no it isn't.

Chris   Oh yes it is.

Repeat and vamp. Hopefully the audience will join in.

Yes! It is! It is! Of course it is. To me it is. This is not
a pantomime.

Robert   Yes it is.

Chris   NO IT ISN'T! . . . But hold, men! What's this?

Cab-sound effect plays.

A cab.

Dennis   Oh no it isn't.

Chris   Yes it is. It is. I don't know why it is, but it is. But also
there's this. Something strange! Odds, bods, hammer and
tongs! There's . . . smoke . . . coming out of this tree stump.
Lots of smoke . . . So much smoke that I can't see the . . .

Suddenly smoke starts to pour out of one of the tree stumps.

There it is – the smoke.

Beat.

(*Prompts.*) A chimney, Captain!

Dennis   A chimney, Captain?

Chris   Listen Cecco! Tis plain they live here, among the
trees and underneath the ground!

Robert (*unintelligible*)   What's your plan, Captain? Shall we
hop down the chimney and fright them all?

Chris   Not so hasty, Starkey! It would be foolish to try and
fight Pan on his own ground. The lagoon isn't far from here,
we'll use our prisoner Tiger Lily to lure them there and set a
trap. Eh, Cecco?

The smoke eclipses them completely.

Francis   It is the wickedest and prettiest plan I ever heard!

Robert (*unintelligible*)   Most wicked and most pretty, Captain Hook! You are a true pirate indeed.

Chris   Now, men, do you see the track back to the shore?

Francis   Aye, Cap'n, I see it as clear as day.

Trevor *enters with a large flattened cardboard box and begins flapping it to clear the smoke. He hits* **Chris** *over the head with it by accident.*

Chris   Starkey, follow it! Get back to the *Jolly Roger* and row Tiger Lily to the lagoon.

We see that **Robert** *has lost his parrot puppet, but is still holding his hand up.*

Chris   Put her out on Marooner's Rock as bait and we'll nab Pan when he tries to save her.

Robert   Aye, Cap'n.

He and **Francis** *rush off. The smoke clears.* **Trevor** *exits.*

Chris   A fine plan, Smee. Shake hands on't!

Dennis *shakes* **Chris**'s *hook, which comes off again.* **Dennis** *exits with the hook to the stage right side.*

Chris   Avast belay, when I appear
By fear they're overtook,
Naught's left upon your bones when you
Have shaken claws with Hook!

He holds up his empty hand. He makes a hook shape with his index finger and exits upstage centre. **Francis** *is quickly slid on in his underwear, half changed out of his Cecco costume.*

Francis   And so the dastardly pirates set off with evil intent. Our story now follows Peter and Wendy to the enchanted lagoon.

The stage revolves again to reveal the nursery set. **Annie** *dressed as Tiger Lily sits on the floor eating a packet of Wotsits. The music stops and the lights come up.*

Francis   There are many mermaids here and it is the end of a long and playful day.

The music plays and the set revolves back the other way revealing **Chris**, **Robert** *and* **Trevor** *trying to lift the trees off* **Lucy**. **Trevor** *is frantically using his buzz saw. They realise the audience can see them and drop the tree back onto* **Lucy**. *The set continues to revolve to reveal the lagoon. Water-like fabric hangs across the stage and a large rock is in the centre.* **ASM**s *rush across the stage with a large blue cloth to represent the water. The moon from the rooftops is held up awkwardly above the set.* **Jonathan** *and* **Sandra** *stand centre,* **Jonathan** *mimes playing his panpipes. The Neverland music transforms into* **Jonathan***'s panpipe playing.* **Max** *glides across the stage on roller-skates dressed as a mermaid.* **Dennis** *then glides across the other way, also dressed as a mermaid. Finally they both glide in at the same time and crash into each othere. They fall over and crawl off together.*

Francis   The sun's rays have persuaded her to give them another five minutes for one more race over the waters before she gathers them up and lets in the moon.

Sandra   Oh, Peter! Mermaids! I would so love to catch one.

Jonathan *begins his line but the panpipe recording hasn't finished.*

Jonathan   Mermaids are fri . . .

He resumes playing his panpipes. The recording finishes.

Mermaids are frightfully dangerous creatures, Wendy. Stay close, I'll show you.

Francis   And with that Peter and Wendy dived down to the bottom of the twilight lagoon.

Lagoon music begins. The company enter all in black with fish and other assorted sea creatures and perform a UV sequence. One actor inflates a balloon decorated as a puffer fish. They accidentally let it go and it flies off. Some fish are accidentally assembled into a phallic shape.

UV models of Peter and Wendy float in. One of Wendy's eyes falls off. **Annie** *and* **Chris** *then enter with a UV mermaid which they make* *swim around in front of Peter and Wendy. The head suddenly falls off and* **Annie** *tries to put it back on. She struggles and bumps into* **Robert** *whose sea creature also breaks. The sea creatures end up mismatched (i.e. mermaid's body with crab's head, etc.). There is some bickering through the darkness and suddenly the main lights snap on and the whole cast are seen dressed completely in black with their props on rods, etc.* **Chris** *motions for the lights to come down. They do and the UV creatures all rush offstage. The lights come back up.*

Sandra   Oh, Peter. I've never seen anything quite like that before.

Jonathan   Nor have I.

Sandra   What is this place, Peter?

Jonathan   This is Marooner's Rock. It is a fearfully important rock. Sailors are marooned here when their captain leaves them and sails away. When the tide is full the rock is covered with water and the sailor drowns.

We hear **Dennis** *(as Mr Smee, still without his headset),* **Robert** *(as Starkey),* **Francis** *and* **Annie** *(hands tied as Tiger Lily) approaching wearing a cut-out of a canoe around their waists. They move with difficulty.* **Robert** *rows with large oars.*

Robert and **Dennis** *(sing)*   Yo ho! Yo ho!

Jonathan   Pirates! Hide!

He and **Sandra** *hide out of sight as the others enter.*

Robert *and* **Dennis** *(sing)*   Yo ho! Yo ho!
    A merry hour,
    A hempen rope,
    And a hey for Davey Jones! *Yarr!*

Dennis   Tis good to be upon the water, me lubber. Now we must follow the captain's orders –

Trevor *holds up a cue-card.*

Dennis *(reads from a cue-card)*   – and hoist Tiger Lily onto the rock and leave her there to drown.

Robert (*unintelligible*)   Out of the boat and up on the rock with you.

Dennis (*reads from a cue-card*)   Do as he says. Get out of the boat.

Robert *crouches to lower the canoe to the floor.* **Annie** *and* **Dennis** *step out.* **Robert** *stands back up and the side of the boat traps their legs inside. He lowers it again so they can get out.*

Robert   Any last words? Speak!

He turns and hits **Annie** *with the canoe.*

Robert   What have you to say?

Annie   These words shan't be my last as Peter Pan shall save me.

Dennis *reads from another of* **Trevor**'s *cue-cards.*

Dennis   This is a terrible show –

Trevor *turns around the card.*

Dennis (*reads from a cue-card*)   – of cowardice, Tiger Lily. We thought you'd put up more of a fight.

Annie   Brave men do not sneak up on defenceless girls – you are the true cowards.

Dennis (*reads from a cue-card*)   You can't act –

Trevor *turns the card.*

Dennis   – in this way when the Captain arrives. You have a sharp tongue now but you shall tremble at the sight of Hook's impressive arse –

Trevor *turns the card.*

Dennis   – nal of weapons back aboard the *Jolly Roger*.

Sandra   Poor Tiger Lily. Help her, Peter.

Jonathan   Of course, I shall. I'll impersonate Hook. Watch!

A recording of **Chris***'s voice plays as* **Jonathan** *mouths the words.*

Chris (*over the speakers*)   Ahoy there, you lubbers!

Dennis (*reads from a cue-card*)   Tis the captain. He must be swimming out to us! *(Calls out.)* Just bringing Tiger Lily up onto the shore, Cap'n.

Chris (*over the speakers*)   Set her free.

Dennis (*reads from a cue-card*)   But, Cap'n, it was your orders to bring her to Marooner's Rock.

Chris (*over the speakers*)   My orders? Nonsense! Release her, you blithering imbeciles! Cut her free!

Robert (*unintelligible*)   Aye, Cap'n!

He goes to untie **Annie***'s hands, but knocks her over by accident; he turns back and knocks* **Dennis** *over.*

Robert   Aye, aye, Cap'n! I'll cut her free!

He tries to get out of the canoe but finds he is stuck. He tries to tell **Dennis** *to release* **Annie** *himself, but what he's saying remains unintelligible – 'Why don't you cut her free, Smee?!', 'I can't set her free, I'm stuck in the boat.' etc.* **Dennis** *doesn't understand.* **Robert** *finally gives up and turns back to* **Annie***, knocking* **Dennis** *over again. He turns again, hitting* **Annie***.* **Dennis** *stands up,* **Robert** *turns back and knocks him forward into the blue fabric which pulls the* **ASM** *and* **Trevor** *onto the stage. They quickly rush back into the wings pulling the fabric taut and sending* **Dennis** *flying back up.* **Robert** *finally manages to get the knife to* **Annie***, who shows her hands to not be tied.*

Robert (*just decipherable*)   She's free, Cap'n!

Annie *runs offstage right.*

Chris (*calls from offstage*)   I'm swimming out to you, boys!

Chris (*as Captain Hook*) *and* **Francis** (*as Cecil*) *enter, clearly seeing* **Annie***.*

Chris   Now where is Tiger Lily?

Dennis (*reads from a cue-card*)   That's alright, captain, we let her go.

Chris   Let her go?!

Dennis (*reads from a cue-card*)   But t'was your own orders, Captain.

Chris   You blundering blockheads, I said no such thing.

Francis   But if you didn't give the orders, Cap'n, who did?

Chris   Perhaps it be the dark spirits that haunt this here lagoon, Starkey.

Robert   Spirits, Cap'n?

He turns the boat and **Dennis** *ducks it.* **Robert** *accidentally hits* **Dennis** *with one of the oars. Eerie lagoon music starts.*

Chris   Spirit! Dost hear me?

Chris (*over the speakers*)   I hear you!

Robert (*over the speakers*)   Cut. Alright, Chris, that's fine. Now get out I want to record my audition tapes.

Trevor *hits the desk and the recording cuts out.*

Chris   Who are you, stranger? Speak!

Chris (*over the speakers*)   I am James Hook! Captain of the *Jolly Roger*!

Chris   Oh no, no! You are not!

Dennis   Oh yes he is!

Chris   *Oh no he's not! He's not.*

Robert (*unintelligible. Puts his hand to his ear.*)   But what's that noise, Cap'n?

Chris   It is a ticking clock! Tis the crocodile!

Max (*as the crocodile*) *rolls on stage, lying on a trolley on wheels. The ticking sound continues.*

Francis   Captain, the crocodile's come to finish you off!

Chris   If you are Hook, then who am I?

Chris (*over the speakers*)   A codfish! A *cod*fish! A codfish!

Robert (*over the speakers*)   Cut. Yes I suppose that'll do. Not very piratey if you ask me.

Chris (*over the speakers*)   Well, at least you can understand what I'm saying.

Robert (*over the speakers*)   Lacks authenticity. Are we done for the day?

Chris (*over the speakers*)   Actually, Robert, there's something I wanted to talk to you about.

Robert (*over the speakers*)   Oh is it Dennis? He doesn't know a single line!

Chris (*over the speakers*)   No it's not that. I'm concerned about Jonathan and Sandra.

Robert (*over the speakers*)   Oh absolutely, their behaviour is just lewd!

Chris (*over the speakers*)   Exactly. Jonathan's playing Peter Pan and Sandra's playing Wendy, they can't be sleeping together.

Robert (*over the speakers*)   He's supposed to be the boy who wouldn't grow up, not the boy who couldn't keep it in his pants.

Jonathan *and* **Sandra** *edge away from each other.*

Robert (*over the speakers*)   And she's just as bad! Flirting with everybody! It's no wonder Max is obsessed with her.

Chris (*over the speakers*)   Is he?

Robert (*over the speakers*)   You've seen the way he looks at her. Pathetic.

Chris (*over the speakers*)   Oh, well, that must be why he keeps asking if he can play Peter Pan, he just wants to get closer to her.

Robert (*over the speakers*)   He didn't? He wants to play Peter?! But Max can't act! He cannot act to save his life. He's terrible as Michael, and the crocodile. He's playing it like a mammal.

Chris (*over the speakers*)   I know he's bad but we need his uncle's money. He's invested forty thousand pounds into this production, Robert! It's the only reason he's here.

Robert (*over the speakers*)   What a loser.

Chris (*over the speakers*)   Oops, left the microphone on –

The recording ends. Silence. All glare at each other. All finally look to **Max**. **Max** *looks to* **Sandra**. **Jonathan** *puts his arms around her.* **Sandra** *looks away from* **Max**. **Max** *slowly exits stage right.* **Chris** *gathers himself.*

Chris   Tis Peter Pan!

Jonathan *leaps out from behind the rocks.*

Jonathan   Tis I!

Chris   Take him dead or alive!

Sandra *embraces* **Jonathan**.

Sandra   Do be careful, Peter!

Chris   Come and face me, Pan!

Dramatic fight music starts to build.

Jonathan   I shall, old and weary Hook!

Chris   You are no match for my might, blade and hook, Pan!

Jonathan   *En guard*, Captain Hook!

The fight begins, swift and slick. **Jonathan** *starts flying higher and higher around* **Chris**. *The water-like fabric is accidentally torn down and the others get tangled in it.*

Chris   Foolish Pan!

Jonathan   Take that, you fiend!

Chris   Vainglorious boy! I shall split your bones with my hook!

Jonathan   Nothing ever hurts me! I'm Peter Pa –

He suddenly starts to shake wildly on his fly line, jerking up and down.

Jonathan   I'm Peter . . . Pa . . . I'm Peter . . . Pa . . . Pet . . . Pa . . . Nothing ever hurts me! I'm Peter Paaan!

He shoots up out of sight into the rig, screaming.

Chris   You'll die by my blade, Pan!

Jonathan   To die will be an awfully big adventuuuuure!

We see his body suddenly drop from the rig straight down onto the stage. A large banner falls down into view reading 'JACK AND THE BEAN' with a picture of **Robert** *smiling dressed as 'Jack' shrugging and holding one single bean. Music cuts out. Silence.*

Chris   Interval!

Blackout. Tabs. House lights and music.

Act Two

The revolve is set back to the forest scene. During the interval a table with benches and some stools has been set centre-stage.

Robert *enters from the wings.*

Robert   Welcome back, ladies and gentlemen. Chris has asked me to come out as his co-director –

Chris (*off*)   Assistant director!

Robert   Thank you, and he's asked me to stall for a few mome . . .

Chris (*off*)   *Speak!*

Robert   To *speak* for a few moments before we resume. Chris is just finishing up dealing with some concerned parents and the paramedics. I am pleased to report that little Lucy is perfectly . . . alive.

Now, I do apologise for the technical issues we've been experiencing. Apparently we are running too many electrical appliances through the theatre, including the revolving stage, all the lighting and sound equipment, and of course my hairdryers. However, we are confident we have resolved the issue –

Robert (*over the speakers*)   Robert Grove audition tape one. Cockney. *Alright, Guvnor! Up the apples and pears! It's all over me boat race!*

One of my audition tapes there . . . But our sound operator Carol has warned us there is a small chance we may experience some audio interruption and periodic blackouts. Electric torches have been distributed to the front row, so please do be ready to light the stage if necessary. Now before we stopped the more keen-eyed of you will have seen that Peter Pan took a rather nasty unrehearsed fall, obviously he wasn't thinking his happy thoughts. Nor will he be when he regains consciousness and learns of the severities of his injuries, and we are still waiting for him to regain consciousness. However do not fear, we are able to continue and I'm sure you will barely notice the difference.

Besides, Peter Pan's injuries are certainly less severe than those sustained in the first act of our previous production of *Oliver!* When during the number 'Boy for Sale' our portly Mr Bumble tripped back onto one of the frailer workhouse children, crushing him. Regrettably I had parked in the ambulance bay and the paramedics were unable to get to the child and he sadly passed. I cannot help but feel partially responsible for that tragic event, as my vehicle did stop medical help getting to him and also because I was playing Mr Bumble.

Silence.

So, as they say in Hollywood: 'on with the show business'.

The cast once again enter with placards and stand in their line.

Robert   Please put your hands together for . . .

The cast turn around their placards to reveal the words 'A TON OF WET PET CRAP'. They quickly rearrange their placards to spell 'ACT TWO OF PETER PAN'.

Robert   Act Two of *Peter Pan!*

All exit into the wings and the lights come up on the new scene. **Sandra** *(as Wendy) lays dishes of imaginary food out on the table.* **Francis** *is gracefully slid into position on his chair but the wrong way around facing upstage. He throws glitter, realises and turns around to begin his narration.*

Francis   We have now reached the evening which was to be known among them as the night of nights, because of its adventures and their upshot. The day, as if quietly gathering its forces, had been almost uneventful and now the children were just about to return to Wendy for their evening meal.

> The meal happened to be an imaginary one,
> With nothing whatever on the table;
> Not a mug, nor a crust, nor knives.
> However, Wendy called the Lost Boys to dinner,
> As if for the greatest feast of their lives.

He holds onto the back of his chair and is slid off gesturing to the stage as the lights come up.

Sandra   Come along, boys! Michael!

Max *appears from behind a tree.*

Max   Yes, Wendy!

Sandra   John!

Dennis *appears, now wearing his headset again.*

Dennis (*holds headset*)   Yes, Wendy!

Sandra   Tootles!

Lucy *hobbles on in crutches, even more terrified than before.*

Lucy   Y-y-y-y-y . . .

Sandra   It's time for dinner!

Dennis   Oh, I do love Neverland! (*Holds headset.*) And now for the shipping forecast.

Max   I hear this evening's meal is imaginary.

Sandra   So it can be anything you want it to be.

All   Anything?

Sandra (*sings*)   You can have steak or salami,
   You can have chestnuts or cheese,
   The only thing to remember
   Is the magic word . . .

All   What?

Sandra   Please!

Max (*spoken*)   So I can have anything I can think of?

Sandra (*spoken*)   Of course!

Max   I could have lobster or lettuce.

Sandra   You could have pastry or pies.

Max   I could have dumplings or damsons.

Dennis (*holds headset*)   Your taxi has arrived!

Dance begins for the chorus.

Sandra   With give and take then you can make,
  Whatever you can conceive,
  With faith and trust and fairy dust,
  And the world of make-believe.

As the chorus begins the **ASM**s, **Annie** *and* **Francis** *join in the dance.*

All   With give and take then we can make,
  Whatever we can conceive,
  With faith and trust and fairy dust,
  And the world of make-believe.

Max (*spoken*)   But Wendy, where's Peter?

Sandra (*spoken*)   This is Neverland, Michael; he could be anywhere you want him to be! (*Sings.*) He could be fighting off pirates.

Max   Or chasing a horse!

Sandra   He could be riding a star.

Francis   Impossible!

Sandra   Of course!

Max   I could be a steam engine driver.

Annie   Or a carnival clown.

Sandra   You could be a prince fighting dragons.

Dennis (*holds headset*)   Shots fired. Suspect is down!

Max   I'll be a warrior winning the war!

Annie   I'll be a lawyer learning the law!

Sandra   I'll be a pastor protecting the poor!

All climb up onto chairs.

Dennis (*holds headset*)   Lady in red!

Sandra *takes off* **Dennis**'s *headset and throws it aside. The music shifts to a tap-dance break.* **Lucy** *struggles to tap with her broken foot.*

All   With give and take then we can make,
    Whatever we can conceive,
    With faith and trust and fairy dust,
    With sticks and stones and bags of bones,
    With ups and downs and all arounds,
    With hops and skips and broken bits.

A brief break where **Robert** *appears as the shadow and reprises his dance. He accidentally breaks through one of the steps on the ladder and gets stuck. We snap back to the main song.*

Sandra   With courage

Dennis   Honour!

Max   Valour!

Annie   Speed!

Sandra   Heroes!

Max   Villains!

Sandra   Goblins!

Annie   Greed!

Sandra   Princes!

Francis   Wizards!

Sandra   Sandstorms!

Max   Blizzards!

Dennis   Action!

Annie   Fighting!

Max   Damsels!

Dennis   Biting!

All   Whatever you can conceive!
  And the world of make believe!
  And the world of make believe!!

Robert *finally pulls his foot out of the broken stair and stands up quickly, accidentally hitting* **Lucy** *in the face with the back of his head. She falls through the door out of sight. The song finishes and the group create a large final tableau.* **Annie**, **Francis** *and the* **ASM**s *skip off.*

Max   I do so love it here.

Sandra   How wonderful!

Max   Oh, I wish we could stay here for ever.

Sandra   Michael, you must not forget we have a mother and father waiting for us back at home. We must not forget their feelings, and Nana's, and Lisa's. Think of all their unhappiness with their children flown away. Think of the empty beds!

Oh, I can hear Peter outside. Quickly all of you, you know how he likes you to meet him.

Trevor *suddenly flies in clutching a script and wearing odd elements of the Peter Pan costume: hat, belt, panpipes, etc. He looks terrified.*

Trevor (*reads stage direction from script*)   Peter enters.

Sandra   Peter, you're back.

Max   Any adventures, Peter?

Trevor   I battled with two tigers and a dozen pirates.

Sandra   How exciting.

Trevor   I love adventures, Wendy! *(Reads stage direction.)* Peter flies around the room, showboating and full of mirth.

He is jerked erratically back and forth around the stage, with the harness causing him a lot of pain.

Sandra   Oh, Peter! No one flies better than you!

Dennis *(holds headset)*   Stop showing off and tell us what happened.

Trevor   Very well. Peter lands nimbly and addresses the others.

He plummets down onto the floor heavily.

It was a dark and windy night down by the lagoon; the rain lashed down onto – Wendy suddenly interrupts him.

Sandra   *Peter*! This sounds wonderful, but first you must have your dinner.

She gives **Trevor** *a knife and fork. He sits down at the table and begins to eat.*

Trevor   Peter begins to eat Tinker Bell. (**Trevor** *misreads where the full stop is in the sentence.*) has behaved most oddly since her return.

Sandra   Perhaps she is angry with me?

Trevor   Fairies have to be one thing or the other because being so small they have room for only one feeling at a time.

He slowly begins to fly up from his seat. He tries to resist and carry on eating. Throughout the dialogue he continues to rise.

Sandra   I fear Tinker Bell is jealous of me.

Trevor   Why should she be jealous?

He clings to the table. He struggles to read from the script and hold all of his props.

Girls are so puzzling; Tiger Lily is just the same. Looks at Wendy seriously for a moment.

He looks sharply at **Sandra**.

Sandra   The three of us do worry about you, Peter.

Trevor   But, Wendy, there is nothing to worry about! No one knows Neverland better than I and I cannot help being at the centre of adventures.

Sandra   But it sounds awfully dangerous, Peter. You are careful out there aren't you?

Trevor *drops down to the floor heavily.*

Trevor   Don't worry, Wendy, nothing ever hurts me; I'm Peter Pan.

Sandra   Peter, I do fear for you though, the world can be such a frightening place. What if Captain Hook were to capture you? I couldn't bear to see you die.

Trevor   Don't worry, Wendy. Peter flies up onto the table.

He begins to climb onto the table.

To die will be an awfully big adventure –

As he steps up a loose plank of wood shoots up and hits him in the face, knocking him unconscious. The Peter Pan hat lands on the table. **Trevor** *hangs in the air. He is then slowly winched offstage. All the remaining cast look at each other and try to think of what to do.* **Sandra** *calls* **Robert** *on. He enters, softly sings 'Boy for sale . . .' to himself and backs away and exits.* **Dennis** *reaches for the hat but is interrupted by the sound of radio feedback.*

Dennis (*holds headset*)   Not you Dennis. Back away.

Dennis *exits.*

Max *takes the hat. Throughout the rest of the scene he plays the role of Peter Pan very well.*

Max   When you die you fly off over the waters and the stars guide your way.

Sandra   Peter . . . The stars do look beautiful in Neverland.

Max   Stars are beautiful, but they may not take an active part in anything, they must just look on for ever. It is a punishment put on them for something they did so long ago that no star now knows what it was. So the older ones have become glassy eyed and seldom speak by their winking, but the little ones still wonder.

Sandra   Oh, Peter.

Max *picks up the panpipes from the floor.*

Max   I do so love adventures.

Max *goes to play the panpipes but the wrong sound cue is played. They listen again in horror.*

Chris (*over the speakers*)   Sound cue recording twenty-one. Panpipes. Take one.

The sound of air being blown through the panpipes.

Chris (*over the speakers*)   Ah. Right. How do you . . . Where's that handbook? Mother, did you move my panpipes handbook?

The sound of the door being opened.

Chris (*over the speakers*)   Oh, Hello, Max.

Max (*over the speakers*)   Hi.

We hear the door close.

Chris (*over the speakers*)   What can I do for you?

Max (*over the speakers*)   Sorry, I just wanted to ask about Peter Pan again.

Chris (*over the speakers*)   Max, we have been over this. You have lot's to do . . . you're playing Michael Darling *and* the crocodile.

Max (*over the speakers*)   But no one likes the crocodile. Everyone likes Peter and . . . Peter gets to do all the fun stuff.

Chris (*over the speakers*)   Like what?

Max (*over the speakers*)   Well, he . . . you know, he gets to kiss Wendy.

Chris (*over the speakers*)   You want to kiss Sandra?

Max (*over the speakers*)   Maybe . . .

Chris (*over the speakers*)   You know she's in a relationship with Jonathan?

Max (*over the speakers*)   Yes! Because he is playing Peter.

Chris (*over the speakers*)   I don't think he'd appreciate . . .

Max (*over the speakers*)   I think I'm in love with Sandra.

Beat.

Chris (*over the speakers*)   Well, that's neither here nor there and certainly no reason to recast . . .

Max (*over the speakers*)   I keep dreaming about her though, Chris.

Chris (*over the speakers*)   Alright, thank you, Max. Now if you don't mind . . .

Max (*over the speakers*)   She's my soulmate.

Chris (*over the speakers*)   Max. If you don't mind I need to finish recording the panpipes.

Max (*over the speakers*)   Oh okay. Er . . . Sorry.

Sound of **Max** *leaving and closing the door.*

Chris (*over the speakers*)   Note: don't use take one.

The recording ends. The whole cast are staring at **Max***. A long silence.* **Max** *plays a few notes on the panpipes.*

Max   I . . . I . . .

Francis *is suddenly fired out onto the stage alarmingly quickly. He falls off the chair but hurriedly stands up and throws glitter. The rest of the cast freeze.*

Francis   But little did Peter, Wendy or the Lost Boys know that up upon the ground above their home Hook, leading his crew, lurked among the trees waiting for them to come out into the night.

Chris (*as Hook*) *leans around a tree looking menacing. His hook has been firmly gaffer-taped to his arm.*

Francis   Down in Peter's hideout,
   Wendy began to understand,
   It was time for her, John and Michael
   To fly home from Neverland.

The chair is whizzed off again just as he goes to sit down. He falls, recovers and exits.

Sandra   Peter, if you would come back with me I'm sure my mother and father would adopt you.

Max   No, Wendy, I flew back once to see my mother but the window was barred and she had forgotten about me and there was another little boy asleep in my bed.

Sandra   Are you sure mothers are like that?

Max   Yes.

Sandra   Peter, what are your exact feelings for me?

A sudden burst of loud panpipe music plays, followed by a burst of 'The World of Make Believe!' We then hear the recording skip with dialogue from different sections of the conversation.

Chris (*over the speakers*)   Take one. Panpip . . .

Robert (*over the speakers*)   Max can't act.

Max (*over the speakers*)   . . . in love with Sandra . . .

Chris (*over the speakers*)   . . . neither here nor ther . . .

Max (*over the speakers*)   I keep dreaming about her . . . dreaming about her . . . dreaming about her . . . dreami . . . She's my soulmate . . . soulmate . . . in love with Sandra . . . In love . . . dreaming about her . . . soulmate . . . oulmate . . . oulmate . . .

Robert (*over the speakers*)   It's all over me boat race!

The recording cuts out. **Max** *stands in silence looking at* **Sandra** *who looks back blankly.*

Max   My feelings are those of a devoted son, Wendy.

Sandra   I thought so. And in that case I must leave at once (*calling to offstage*). Come all of you, fetch your things. If you will come with me my mother and father shall adopt you all. It will only mean having a few more beds in the drawing room. Oh, Peter, say you'll come with us.

Max   No. I shall stay here and always be a little boy and have fun.

Sandra   Then you must . . . kiss me goodbye, Peter.

Max *reaches into the brim of his hat and produces the thimble.*

Sandra   Oh, Peter. I meant a real kiss.

Max   A real kiss?

Sandra   You do not know what a real kiss is?

Max   No. I do not.

Sandra   Then I shall show you.

Jonathan *appears at the side of the stage.* **Sandra** *runs past* **Max** *to* **Jonathan** *and kisses him.* **Max** *stands there.*

Jonathan   This is a real kiss?

Sandra   Yes, Peter, a real kiss.

Dennis *re-enters pushing* **Lucy** *in a wheelchair.*

Jonathan   It's time for you to go now, no fuss, no blubbering. I hope your mother is happy to see you again. Be careful you don't run into pirates. Or that crocodile (*To* **Max**.) that nobody likes.

He takes back his hat and the acorn. **Max** *walks off slowly.*

Sandra   Peter, you will remember to take your medicine won't you?

Jonathan   I won't forget.

Sandra   Goodbye, Peter.

Jonathan   Goodbye, Wendy. Goodbye, boys.

All   Goodbye.

Chris (*still as Captain Hook*) *and* **Robert** (*as pirate Starkey*) *appear in the doorway.* **Francis**'s *chair comes out without him on it. He rushes on and sits down. Hook's theme music begins.*

Francis   The travellers start upon their journey, little witting that Hook had issued his silent orders: his men to hide in wait among the trees. As the children walk by they are plucked, trussed and gagged.

As the narration continues the cast enact the kidnapping in silence. **Robert**, **Chris** *and* **Dennis** *find that the wheelchair cannot fit through the gap in the trees where they are supposed to exit. They awkwardly lift* **Lucy** *in her wheelchair up and through a larger space.*

Francis   Hook signed to his dogs to be gone and they departed through the forest. The screams and cries lost to Peter as he had fallen asleep in his chair dreaming of a boy who is never here, nor anywhere, the only boy who could beat him. Once the pirates had carried the children a few more paces into the night Hook crept into the clearing.

    And with stealth, cunning, guile and craft
    He added poison to the medicine draught.

He is retracted on his chair. **Chris** *creeps to the front of the stage standing in front of* **Jonathan**.

Chris   Now where is Peter Pan? *Where* is Peter Pan?

Audience shout 'He's behind you' . . . **Chris** *tries to continue his line but is overwhelmed by the audience participation.*

Chris   I know he is! *I know he is* . . . you've got to let me find him.

He looks around.

There he is.

He picks up a small bottle.

Poison . . . medicine . . .

He struggles to open the bottle of poison with his hook. Eventually he manages it. He pours his vial of poison into the medicine bottle and leaves it on the table in front of **Jonathan**. *If the audience boo him* **Chris** *improvises the line 'If I was to boo you . . . you wouldn't like it . . .' Tinker Bell is heard and her light flutters in and then out through the stage left door.* **Annie** *enters from the stage left door and walks in, lit up on her cable.* **Jonathan** *wakes up.*

Jonathan   Wendy? Tink! Tinker Bell! What's the matter?

Annie *jingles her bells.*

Jonathan   What's that? Wendy and the boys captured by pirates? I'll rescue her! Where's my dagger?

Annie *jingles her bells.*

Jonathan   That? It's just my medicine.

Annie *jingles her bells.*

Jonathan   Poisoned? Who could have poisoned it? I promised I would take it and I will.

Annie *jingles her bells fiercely and tries to take the medicine bottle.* **Jonathan** *struggles to get it back. During the struggle* **Trevor** *enters (now bandaged) and unspools more cable for* **Annie** *who gets her leg caught around it.*

Jonathan   Tink! No! What are you doing? That's *my* medicine! Stop drinking it! Stop it! Stop it!

Annie *finally takes the bottle and undoes the lid, but then trips on the cable around her leg and spills the poison all over herself and the power pack of the extension lead. An electrical fizz is heard and her fairy lights suddenly shine very brightly. A sudden pop is heard and the whole stage is plunged into darkness. Sparks fly up. Silence.*

Whispering is heard and then the sound of the power rebooting and the lights coming back on. **Annie** *is on the floor unconscious, her fairy lights out.* **Jonathan** *tentatively approaches her.* **Trevor** *steps into view looking at her.*

Jonathan   Tink . . .? You drunk it . . . It was poisoned and you drunk it to save my life . . . Tink . . .? Tink are . . . are you alright? Tink?

He looks into the wings, scared, and signals for help.

Chris . . .

Chris *enters and goes over to help.*

Chris   Is she breathing? Who's the first aider?

Robert   Who's the first aider?

Trevor   She's the first aider.

Other cast members enter. Vamp. The mood becomes quite serious. We hear the word 'electrocuted'.

Sandra   Robert, call an ambulance . . . and move your car.

Lucy *enters in the wheelchair and tries to speak up.*

Lucy   W . . . w . . . we have t . . . t . . . to believe in f . . . f . . . fairies.

Robert   Not now, Lucy, this is serious!

Lucy   I b . . . b . . . believe in fairies.

Robert   Thank you, that's enough!

Lucy *stands up with difficulty and begins to clap.*

Lucy   I b . . . b . . . believe in fairies.

Robert   Grow up, Lucy!

Max *joins in.*

Lucy *and* **Max**   I b-b-believe in fairies.

Dennis, **Francis**, **Trevor** *and* **Sandra** *join in as well, one by one. Gradually the cast and audience begin clapping and chanting 'I b-b-believe in fairies'. Eventually even* **Chris** *and* **Robert** *join in but* **Jonathan** *does not. As the shouting reaches a peak* **Annie** *suddenly springs up and gasps for air. The cast freeze, shocked.*

Chris   Positions!

All but **Annie** *and* **Jonathan** *exit.*

Jonathan   Well done! Well done! Thank you! You've saved Tinker Bell! And now to rescue Wendy! Come on, Tink! To the pirate ship! It's Hook or me this time!

'Yo ho, yo ho a pirates life' begins to play on the speakers and the set begins to slowly revolve to reveal the lagoon set, now containing the deck of the Jolly Roger *complete with cannon, plank, large sails and a pirate flag.* **Chris** *(as Hook),* **Francis** *(as Cecco) and* **Robert** *(as Starkey) stand holding many guns, knives, etc.* **Sandra** *and* **Dennis** *(as John) are tied to the mast.*

All *(sing)*   Yo ho! Yo ho!
    Yo ho, the pirate life,
    The flag of skull and bones,
    A merry hour, a hempen rope
    And hey for Davy Jones!

    Avast, belay, yo ho, heave to,
    A-pirating we go,
    And if we're parted by a shot,
    We're sure to meet below.

    Yo ho, the pirate life,
    The flag of skull and bones,
    A merry hour, a hempen rope,
    And hey for Davy Jones!

    A-sailing on the seven seas,
    What better life is there?
    And any honest Jack or John
    Had better best beware!

Yo ho, the pirate life,
The flag of skull and bones,
A merry hour, a hempen rope,
And hey for Davy Jones!

There's not a sea we never sailed,
Or drink we never drank,
And any lubber says not so,
We'll see him walk the plank!

Yo ho, the pirate life,
The flag of skull and bones,
A merry hour, a hempen rope,
And hey for Davy Jones!

Come raise the mast and swab the deck,
And let the anchor sink,
We'll stab and kill and plunder too,
And then we'll have a drink.

Yo ho, the pirate life,
The flag of skull and bones,
A merry hour, a hempen rope,
And hey for Davy Jones!

We have no wives; we have no woes,
Well never show no fear,
You do what you must do to live,
When you're a buccaneer!

Yo ho, the pirate life,
The flag of skull and bones,
A merry hour, a hempen rope,
And hey for Davy Jones!

Ye scurvy dog, give me your gold,
And then we'll hoist the sail,
Remember if you try to squeal,
A dead man tells no tales!

Yo ho, the pirate life,
The flag of skull and bones,
A merry hour, a hempen rope
And hey for Davy Jones!

Hey!

The following action happens throughout the song. The pirate ship set doesn't stop and the full scene is carried back off around the other side of the stage and the next segment of the set comes around: the nursery. **Lucy** *is in the wheelchair, her leg still bandaged.*

Trevor *is making her sign documents titled 'LEGAL DISCLAIMER'. A* **Paramedic** *is treating her at the same time. They all slowly realise the revolve is broken and look out at the audience, and the set continues to revolve revealing the forest set where* **Jonathan** *is kissing* **Annie** *(still as Tinker Bell). They realise they've been seen but then go back to kissing.*

The pirate ship comes around again, the scene exactly the same as it was before, the group confident that the revolve will stop this time. It doesn't stop. The pirate ship continues back around and the nursery set is revealed again. This time **Trevor** *is alone. He has opened a fuse box in the floor with wires coming out of it and is desperately trying to fix the problem. The set keeps revolving to reveal the forest scene with* **Annie** *and* **Jonathan** *kissing and* **Sandra** *looking on from the side. She slaps* **Jonathan**, *jumps on his back and starts hitting him with his hat.* **Annie** *rushes off. The pirate ship comes back around and the scene is exactly the same as it was before except* **Lucy** *is now there too. The group are hopeful that the revolve will stop this time. It doesn't stop. The nursery is revealed again, where* **Trevor** *is still kneeling at the fuse box. He hits it with a hammer and sparks suddenly erupt from the it.* **Dennis** *enters through the ship/ nursery door and uses strips of gaffer tape to try and stop the revolving stage. The forest is revealed again.* **Sandra** *and* **Jonathan** *having a huge argument.* **Sandra** *hits* **Jonathan** *with a bindle.* **Jonathan** *tries to kiss* **Sandra**; *she pushes him away and runs off.*

The set keeps turning revealing the pirate ship once more. **Chris** *is alone, still trying to create a full scene by himself. The pirate ship continues around to reveal* **Trevor**, **Robert** *and* **Dennis** *having an argument over the fuse box. They notice they have been seen and form the image of a pirate ship using disregarded props and bits of set from the nursery.* **Trevor** *abandons the fuse box and runs* *through to the forest section as that comes around past* **Jonathan** *sitting miserably alone (maybe drinking whisky from a hip flask) and rushes offstage left to pick up a broom.*

As the pirate ship comes around again and the song finishes **Trevor** *wedges the broom in the side of the revolve so it stops turning. The broom budges and bends under the strain. The moon is held up above the set.*

Chris How still the night is. Nothing sounds alive.

The car-horn sound effect is played again.

Chris A CAB! Why is there a cab in the sea?! Revenge will soon be mine.

The car-horn sound effect is played again.

Chris GOD!! CAROL!!

Robert (*over the speakers*) Audition tape seventy-two. Arrogant man. Oh I'm Chris Bean. I'm directing a play and playing Captain Hook at the same time. Look at me with my thin hands.

Recording cuts out. **Chris** *looks at* **Robert**.

Chris This is my hour of triumph.

Sandra Save us, Peter!

Chris Quiet, you dogs, or I'll cast anchor in you! Now, you blithering scurs, you have to make your choice. Will you join my crew? Or will you die tonight in the light of the crescent moon?

The unseen crew member holding the moon quickly snaps it in half and holds one half up.

Sandra We shall none of us ever be pirates.

Chris Is that so, my dear? It'll be the plank for you then. Isn't that right, Mr Smee?

Dennis (*dressed as* **John**) Aye, Captain!

Radio feedback sound.

Dennis   Dennis you're in the wrong costume. That is obviously not a line! You are the worst actor I have ever worked with. I'm leaving. No Carol don't go. I can't do this anymore Gerry I'm forty two. I'm wasting my life working with these people. Carol If you walk out of that door you are not just walking away from this production you are walking away from our marriage. This is a sham of marriage Gerry. You know it. I know it. Even the kids know it. Im sorry. Goodbye. She's gone. She's gone. I can't believe she's gone. Fifteen years of marriage down the toilet. Keep it together Gerry. It looks like you are going to have to step in and save yet another production. Hi Dennis it's Gerry. How you doing little guy? I'm going to be taking over for the rest of the show feeding you your lines, so let's pick it up from the line 'Aye Captain.' Okay. On the count of three. One. Two. Three. Aye Captain!

Chris   Cecco, get the plank ready.

Francis   Aye, sir!

He jumps down from a door in the ship, hitting the deck a little hard and sending the whole ship tipping forwards and the whole cast rolling to the bottom.

Chris   Bring the first prisoner to the plank, Starkey.

Robert   Aye!

Sandra   Be brave, Tootles!

Robert *unsurely looks at* **Lucy**.

Robert   Tootles, Captain?

Chris   . . . Tootles.

Dennis (*holds headset*)   Very well! Up onto the plank with you, Tootles!

He pushes **Lucy** *in the wheelchair up towards the plank. It rolls back down.*

Chris   Walk to the end and meet your fate, vile child!

Dennis *tries again but the chair rolls back down again. The others slowly climb up the tilted ship to level it out but end up going too far, sending it tipping the other way and catapulting* **Lucy** *off the ship who is caught by* **Trevor.** **Trevor** *exits with* **Lucy** *in his arms taking the wheelchair with him.*

Chris   There's none can save him now.

Jonathan (*off*)   There is one!

Suddenly he swings in on his wire. He knocks down the moon, gets tangled in the Jolly Roger *flag and steps on the crossbeam of the mast, which spins on a pivot and hits him in the face.*

Tis I! Peter Pan, the avenger!

He lands on the front of the ship tipping it back the other way, the cast tumble down it again.

I have come to save you all.

Chris   Pan!

Sandra   Peter!

The cast slowly and cautiously try to rebalance the ship, tentatively saying their lines.

Chris   Cleave him to the brisket.

Dennis (*holds headset*)   Seize him, Cecco! Let's slice his gizzard open.

Francis   Aye, Smee. I'll spill your guts, Pan. Take that.

He very slowly swings his sword.

Jonathan   Down, boys, and at them. Quickly, this way, Wendy.

Sandra   Oh, Peter.

Ticking clock is heard and **Max** *in the crocodile costume enters from the stage left side and prowls around outside the ship.*

Jonathan   Hook! The crocodile is here; he knows your end is near.

Chris   Surround them. This one's mine.

Jonathan   Dark and sinister man. Have at thee.

Chris   Back you pewling spawn.

Dennis (*as John*)   You're mine, Smee! (*As Smee.*) Prepare to die, boy!

Fight sequence begins. **Annie** *enters (as Tinker Bell).* **Jonathan** *fights* **Chris**. **Francis** *fights* **Annie**. **Sandra** *fights* **Robert**. **Dennis** *fights himself.* **Max** *knocks out the broom pinning the revolve as he passes and the revolve begins to turn again. The pirate ship tips back again as the revolve turns sending the cast back down to the floor.*

The nursery set is revealed. **Chris** *climbs over the nursery wall to continue his fight with* **Jonathan**. *The others follow over the wall and start to fight through the nursery staying in view of the audience as the revolve continues to turn.* **Trevor** *again kneels by the fuse box as sparks burst up from it.*

The fighting pairs move through to the forest set as that comes around again. We see an **ASM** *putting warning tape across the broken tree branch.* **Chris** *struggles to reach* **Jonathan** *as he flies above the set getting hit by the walls as they come around on the revolve. We see* **Lucy** *on the floor her bandages loose, now holding a pair of crutches.*

The pirate ship comes back around again. **Chris** *climbs onto the ship, the floor tips and he slides down to the other end.* **Robert** *climbs up the other side and raises the level enough for* **Chris** *to climb onto the nursery wall again.*

As the nursery comes around we see **Trevor** *over by the fuse box. He fiddles with some of the wires, more sparks fly up and suddenly the revolve begins to go faster, the cast having to run faster to keep up with it and desperately try to keep their fights going.* **Sandra** *has managed to jump off the revolve and tries to re-wedge the broom to stop the revolve but it's going too fast.* **Robert** *slides off and grabs onto the wall of the set. He is pulled across the stage by the sheer speed of the revolve. Eventually he lets go and tries to jump back on but can't as it's going too fast. As the forest goes around again we see that the entire forest has been covered in warning tape.*

The revolve speeds up faster. The next time we see the nursery set again **Lucy** *(still on crutches) is now clinging desperately onto the side of the bunk-beds. The top bunk, now reset, falls and traps someone's foot. The rest keep running until they can't any longer and begin holding onto the walls and sides as it begins to whizz around faster and faster. Furniture from the forest and nursery scenes falls over and flies off the revolve.*

Jonathan *manages to grab hold of some rigging to keep himself free. Finally we see* **Trevor** *pull out a large piece of cable from the fuse box in the nursery; a wrenching sound is heard and the revolve begins to slow.* **Chris** *loses his grip and is thrown off the revolve by its momentum and flies into* **Max** *who catches him to his own surprise. The revolve spins to a stop between the nursery and the pirate ship. Stillness.*

Jonathan *loses his grip and swings down towards* **Sandra**. **Max** *sees this, drops* **Chris** *and grabs* **Sandra** *out of the way just before* **Jonathan** *swings wildly across the stage.*

Sandra   You saved me . . . Peter. You saved all of us. You're a hero.

Max *pulls off the head of his crocodile costume.*

Max   I'm not Peter. I'm the crocodile.

Francis *crawls towards the downstage right area. Suddenly the chair shoots out and hits him in the head. He falls unconscious. All the others are stuck or injured.* **Chris** *slumps to the floor, broken, and starts sobbing.* **Lucy** *hobbles unsurely towards the chair discarding her crutches on the way. Slowly she picks up the narrator's storybook. The lights dim and a spotlight comes up.*

Lucy   T . . . Thus . . . perished James Hook, and his crew, devoured by the merciless jaws of the crocodile.

Wendy of course had stood, taking no part in the fight, though now she watched her hero with glistening eyes and when he slept that night she held him tight . . .

Sandra *looks at* **Max**. *Music begins.*

Jonathan   Cast off me hearties! Hoist the sails and let us go home! Obey the orders of Captain Pan!

Lucy   . . . and now sadly it is time to bring an end to our tale, for we must leave Neverland . . .

Annie *re-enters as Tinker Bell and stands with* **Jonathan** *on the ship.*

Lucy   . . . where Peter and Tinker Bell sailed the *Jolly Roger* across the skies and were to have many more adventures.

Jonathan *and* **Annie** *exit.*

Lucy   Tiger Lily returned to her tribe with another story of Marooner's Rock to scare the braves.

Annie *crosses the stage now dressed as Tiger Lily.*

Lucy   But now we must return to that desolate home from which three of our characters had taken heartless flight so long ago.

Dennis, **Max** *and* **Trevor** *gather at the side of the revolve and push it around to fully reveal the nursery again; the furniture is upturned.* **Trevor** *and* **Chris** *help* **Jonathan** *down.* **Trevor** *closes the fuse box and quickly leaves.* **Annie** *is already sitting down on the broken bed as Lisa.*

Lucy   Lisa, the housekeeper, sat by the window, and seeing the children approach ran to fetch her mistress.

Annie *rushes out through the nursery door and immediately re-enters as Mrs Darling.*

Lucy   Mrs Darling looked out at her children and the smile at the corner of her mouth that had withered with grief, brightened. Wendy, John and . . . the crocodile found the window open.

Sandra, **Dennis**, *and* **Max** *enter through the window.* **Max** *helps* **Sandra**.

Lucy   On seeing them Mrs Darling could scarcely speak, such was the emotion that overwhelmed her delicate heart. Mr Darling came rushing in from the yard to celebrate the homecoming of his dear ones.

Chris *enters dressed as Mr Darling, but still with the hook gaffer taped onto his arm. He embraces the children.*

Lucy   And as for the Lost Boys, they were all adopted by the Darlings and for the first time felt the love of a mother. There could not have been a lovelier sight but there was none to see it except a strange boy who was sitting at the window.

Snow falls gently outside the nursery. **Jonathan**, *nicely silhouetted, looks in from the window. Music begins to play. A ladder appears in the window and* **Robert** *climbs up dressed as the shadow. He leans on the windowsill behind Peter.*

Lucy   Eventually they would all grow up. Their adventures with Peter Pan and Neverland would become the shadows of memories and it wouldn't take long for them to forget how to fly, even to chase their hats, and of course they would soon cease to believe in fairies.

Robert *falls backwards on his ladder, out of sight. We hear a crash.*

Lucy   But right now the children, Mr and Mrs Darling . . . and the crocodile stood together, united in their newfound bliss, and perhaps it was at this moment they all realised that to live would be an awfully big adventure.

Music swells. Lights fade to black.